Cam and the Sock

Written by Emily Hooton
Illustrated by Cherie Zamazing

Collins

Gock picks a sock.

2

A dot is on the sock.

Pit pat, pit pat.

4

Gock pops!

Cam packs the kit.

Gock naps in a pot.

Cam tips the pot.

Gock dips and pops.

pop!

Cam packs the sock.

:paw: Review: After reading :paw:

Use your assessment from hearing the children read to choose any GPCs, words or tricky words that need additional practice.

Read 1: Decoding

- Turn to page 12 and discuss the meaning of **dips and pops**. Ask: What does Gock do? Encourage the children to use their own words in place of **dips** (e.g. *swoops, drops*) and **pops** (e.g. *disappears with a popping sound*).

- Focus on /c/ sounds. Ask the children to point to the letter or letters that make the /c/ sound in these words:

  Cam   **kit**   **sock**   **picks**

- Challenge the children to read the following words. Ask: Can you blend in your head when you read these words?

  Gock   **pop**   **pot**   **top**

Read 2: Prosody

- Turn to page 4 and ask the children to read the text. Challenge them to sound out the words rhythmically to sound like Gock's footsteps.

- Challenge the children to read page 5, and make the word **pop!** sound like a popping noise. Try different tones (e.g. lower/higher; quieter/louder). Ask: What sounds like a pop?

Read 3: Comprehension

- Turn to pages 8 and 9. Ask: Have you ever lost a sock, or something you need to wear? Encourage the children to talk about their experiences.

- Look together at pages 2–5. Ask: Have you heard stories about fairies taking things before? (e.g. *the tooth fairy*) Discuss some ideas for why Gock takes the sock. (e.g. *for fun, to keep her warm, she likes them*)

- Ask the children to retell the story, using the pages as prompts. Ask questions to draw out more detail, for example:

  o   Which sock did Gock choose?

  o   Where did Gock fall asleep?

  o   Where did Cam put the sock in the end?

- Look at the "I spy sounds" pages (14–15) together. Ask the children to point out as many things as they can in the picture that begin with the /g/ and /o/ sounds. (*glove, glasses, green, Gock, orange, owls, octopuses*)